Around the World

Sports

Margaret C. Hall

Heinemann Library
Chicago, Illinois

Customer Service 888-454-2279

Visit our website at www.heinemannlibrary.com

Designed by Lisa Buckley
Printed in Hong Kong

06 05 04 03 02
10 9 8 7 6 5 4 3 2 1

Library of Congress Cataloging-in-Publication Data
Hall, Margaret, 1947-
   Sports / Margaret Hall.
      p. cm. -- (Around the world)
Summary: Presents an overview of sports played around the world,
mentioning indoor, outdoor, land, water, body, wheeled, along with their
rules and gear.
Includes bibliographical references (p.) and index.
   ISBN 1-58810-478-8 (lib. bdg.)
   1. Sports--Juvenile literature. [1. Sports.] I. Title.
   GV705.4 .H35 2002
   796--dc21
                          2001002472

Acknowledgments
The author and publishers are grateful to the following for permission to reproduce copyright material:

Cover photograph reproduced with permission of Michael S. Yamashita/Corbis

Title page, p.11 Timespace/The Viesti Collection; p.4 RaviShenkhar—Dinodia/The Image Works; p.5
Schiller/The Image Works; p.6 Bob Daemmrich/The Image Works; pp.7, 15 © Nik Wheeler; p.8 Craig
Prentis/Allsport; pp.9, 29 Neil Tingle/Action Plus; p.10 © Cathy Melloan; p.12 Paul A. Souders/Corbis; p.13
Neil Rabinowitz/Corbis; p.14 Jon Burbank/The Image Works; p.16 John Wisden & Co. Ltd.; p.17 © Nancy
Battaglia; p.18 Gunter Marx/Corbis; p.19 Mike King/Corbis; p.20 Stephanie Maze/Corbis; p.21 Le Segretain
Pascal/Corbis Sygma; pp.22, 23 © Victor Englebert; p.24 © Richard T. Nowitz; p.25 Bas Czerwinski/AP
Wide World; p.26 Sovfoto/Eastfoto; p.27 Caroline Penn/Panos Pictures; p.28 Sean Sprague/Panos Pictures

Every effort has been made to contact copyright holders of any material reproduced in this book.
Any omissions will be rectified in subsequent printings if notice is given to the publisher.

The author would like to thank her family—John, Alison, and Jason.

Some words are shown in bold, **like this.** You can find
out what they mean by looking in the glossary.

Contents

Sports Around the World

These children in India are playing an outdoor sport called cricket.

All around the world, people enjoy sports. The kind of sports people play often depends on what the land and **weather** are like where they live.

Boys in the United Arab Emirates race camels.

People once ran or rode animals just to travel quickly. They caught fish just to use as food. Now running, horseback riding, and fishing are sports.

Outdoor Sports

This boy is practicing mountain climbing in Texas.

People play many different sports outside. The kind of sports they play depends on the **weather** where they live.

Skiing is a popular sport in Finland.

Some sports can only be played outside when there is snow or ice. Sports like skiing and ice-skating started in places where it gets very cold.

Indoor Sports

These men in England are playing squash in front of a crowd.

Some sports can be played inside special buildings. These buildings have lots of room for **athletes** to play. There is also room for people to watch them.

People can play water sports all year at an indoor pool.

Inside a **sports arena,** the temperature can be set at a comfortable level. The outside **weather** does not matter. That means many sports can be played all year long.

Sports on Land

A teacher plays basketball with his students in Mexico.

Many sports are played on land. Sports like baseball, football, and soccer are played on fields. Sports like tennis and basketball are played on **courts.**

These Korean girls are having a race.

Some land sports are very fast. People race to see who is best. Other land sports are slow, like golf. Players need time to play carefully.

Water Sports

In New Zealand, people race on their surfboards.

Sports like swimming and surfing started a long time ago. People who lived near water learned to swim to stay safe in the water. Surfing was done just for fun.

This sailboat race is in the Caribbean.

People also like to race **sailboats** and **motorboats** as a water sport. Another water sport is water-skiing. Fast boats pull skiers behind them.

Learning a Sport

This boy in Japan is learning how to hit a baseball. He hits one ball after another, until he gets it right.

People often start to learn a sport when they are young. But they can also keep learning new sports even after they have grown up.

This young girl in Portugal is practicing how to play tennis.

It takes a lot of **practice** to become good at a sport. The more someone plays a sport, the better he or she gets at it.

Rules

Cricket is a sport that has many rules.

Every sport has a set of rules. Rules tell how players should act and what they should do. **Athletes** have to obey these rules.

A referee gets a hockey match started between teams from the United States and Canada.

Some people have the job of making sure players always follow the rules. **Umpires, referees,** and judges tell players if a rule has been broken.

Sports Contests

Two football teams in Canada get ready to start a game.

People often play sports in **teams.** The teams have **contests.** Most of the time one team wins the game. But sometimes they are just for fun.

These children in England are racing to see who is the fastest runner.

Athletes may **compete** to see who is better at a sport. Some athletes do not compete at all. They may play a sport simply because they enjoy it.

Sports Gear

This baseball team is in Puerto Rico.

Some sports **teams** have special clothing. Often, the players on a team wear clothing that looks the same. These **uniforms** show that they are on the team.

Two Ukrainian men compete in a sport called fencing.

Some sports are played with **equipment** like balls, nets, rackets, and even **sabers.** Things like masks and gloves are used to help keep the players safe.

Ball Sports

This soccer team is in Korea.

Many sports are played with balls. Some ball sports look the same but have more than one name. A game called soccer in some places is called football in others.

These children in the Philippines are playing basketball outside.

Ball sports are played inside and outside. They are played on fields and on **courts.** They can be played by **teams** or by just one person.

Sports on Wheels

This boy in Japan likes to compete in races on his bicycle.

Wheels are used for **transportation** and for sports, too. People ride bicycles for **exercise** or to **compete** in races. They ride mountain bikes over rough ground.

This international motorcycle race is in the Netherlands. The two riders shown here are from France and Spain.

For some sports, people race each other on motorcycles or in cars. These races may be held on roads or on **tracks.**

Body Sports

This Russian girl is doing gymnastics.

For some sports, the body is the only **equipment** a player needs. People who do sports like gymnastics and wrestling learn many ways to move their bodies.

The students in this karate class in Azerbaijan are practicing their moves.

Martial arts are sports like judo and karate. They began thousands of years ago as ways to learn self-control. Now martial arts are done all around the world as a sport.

Sports for All

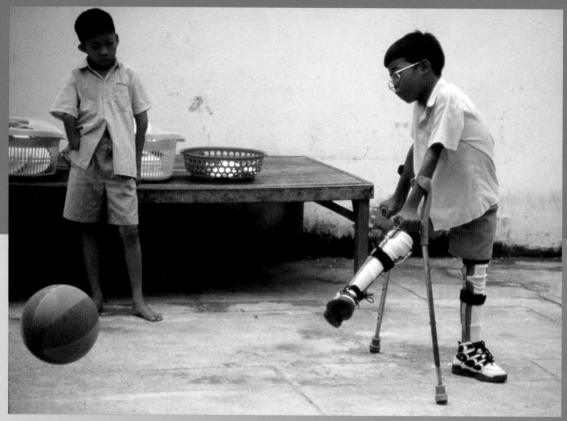

This Cambodian boy plays sports using leg braces and crutches.

People with **disabilities** play sports, too. They may play in wheelchairs or they may use special **equipment.** These **athletes** often **compete** against each other.

Many people come to watch the French Open tennis game.

Around the world, sports are alike in some ways and different in other ways. But, no matter where people live, they enjoy playing and watching sports.

Amazing Sports Facts

✪ More people around the world play soccer than any other sport.

✪ The Olympic Games started thousands of years ago. At first, there was only one sport. People raced to see who was the fastest runner.

✪ Some ice-skaters can go as fast as 35 miles (56 kilometers) per hour. They wear tight clothing and crouch down in order to skate at high speeds.

✪ People play sports with balls made from many different materials. They use balls made of leather, rags, and even twigs!

Glossary

athlete   someone trained in a sport

compete   to take part in a game against another person or team

contest   game against another person or team

court   hard playing surface

disability something that makes it difficult or impossible for a person to do an activity

equipment   things needed to play a sport

exercise   activities that keep a person's body in good shape

martial art   art of self-defense that is often done as a sport

motorboat   boat that is powered by a motor

practice   to do something over and over to get better at it

referee   someone who watches a game to make sure no one breaks the rules

saber   sword used in the sport of fencing

sailboat   boat that is powered by wind blowing against sails

sports arena   building in which sports events take place

team   group of people playing together, usually against another team

tie   score that is the same for two people or two teams

track   round or oval surface for racing

transportation   ways people move from place to place

umpire   someone who decides what to do during a game if players do not agree about something

uniform   clothing that shows that a person belongs to a sports team

weather   what it is like outside, including things like hot or cold air, rain or sun

31

More Books to Read

Ajmera, Maya and Michael J. Regan. *Let the Games Begin!* Watertown, Mass.: Charlesbridge, 2000.

Bizley, Kirk. *Gymnastics.* Chicago: Heinemann Library, 1999.

Bizley, Kirk. *Soccer.* Chicago: Heinemann Library, 1999.

Bizley, Kirk. *Swimming.* Chicago: Heinemann Library, 1999.

Index